For Dad,

With Love

THE POCKET

For Dad,

With Love

G:

Published in 2025
by Gemini Books
Part of Gemini Books Group

Based in Woodbridge and London

Marine House, Tide Mill Way,
Woodbridge, Suffolk IP12 1AP
United Kingdom

www.geminibooks.com

Text and Design © 2025 Gemini Adult Books Ltd
Part of the Gemini Pockets series

Text by Becky Freeth
Cover illustration by Shutterstock/Pattern Talent

ISBN 978-1-80247-303-2

A CIP catalogue record for this book is available from the British Library.

Manufacturer's EU Representative: Eurolink Compliance Limited, 25 Herbert
Place, Dublin, D02 AY86, Republic of Ireland. admin@eurolink-europe.ie

Printed in Poland

10 9 8 7 6 5 4 3 2

Picture Credits: Shutterstock: Angelina Bambina 33, 52; Anna Putina 15, 30, 64, 107,
116, 117; livingpicture 8, 39, 86, 87, 127; Maria Petrishina 35, 44, 50, 55, 82, 83, 90, 91,
100, 114, 115, 120; Olniz 13, 34, 36, 37, 40, 41, 47, 51, 53, 54, 59, 65, 68, 76, 77, 78, 80, 84, 88,
92, 103, 109, 110, 113, 122, 126; Pattern Talent 3, 11, 18, 26, 43, 56, 72, 75, 94, 118; Svetlana
Pyatigorska 4, 22, 49, 78, 79, 92, 93, 98, 111; Victoria Nevzorova 12, 84, 85, 119.

To:

From:

Date:

Contents

Introduction

Dads – what would we do without them? They are the superhero who doesn't wear a cape; our carer, protector and provider. The person we can rely on to fix *anything* (even a broken heart) without expecting anything in return. There are approximately 1.5 billion dads in the world, but to each of us, ours is the number one.

Think of this book as the card that keeps on giving. It's packed with facts, research and typical things that dads say and do (with a few inevitable dad jokes thrown in!). It's our way of saying:

"Thanks, dad. You're the best!"

Chapter One

All About Dads

On Being a Dad

You could be a new dad, or an old one (sorry, Dad!), a grandfather or a father figure, and you would know what it means to be a pillar of the family.

The fact is, fathers are not born, they are made. There is no handbook or entry exam. It's about more than having a child, it's about everything that comes after.

"I cannot think of any need in childhood as strong as the need for a father's protection."

SIGMUND FREUD, *CIVILIZATION AND ITS DISCONTENTS*, 1929

"DAD" IN OTHER LANGUAGES

Irish – *Daid*

Welsh – *Tad*

Spanish – *Papá*

French – *Papa*

Greek – *Bampás*

Filipino – *Tatay*

Dutch – *Pa*

Chinese – *Bà*

Croatian – *Tata*

Danish – *Far*

Hungarian – *Apa*

Portuguese – *Papai*

The Origins of "Dad"

Did you know, the word "Dad" is thought to come from baby talk? "Da-da" is commonly one of the first words recognized by parents, with "da" being one of the easiest consonant sounds for babies to make by using the tongue at the roof of their mouths. Records of the word date back to as early as the sixteenth century and, remarkably, around the world, many abbreviations sound similar.

Unpaid Roles Assigned to Dads:

- ☑ Part-time taxi driver
- ☑ Chief fixer of all broken things
- ☑ King of the BBQ
- ☑ Bear hugger
- ☑ General problem solver
- ☑ Spider/mouse/bird catcher
- ☑ Finder of the lost remote
- ☑ CEO of the sofa
- ☑ Mower of the lawn
- ☑ Sharer of breaking news
- ☑ Amateur comedian
- ☑ Superhero

"The object of love is the best and most beautiful. Try to live up to it."

JOHN STEINBECK, IN A LETTER TO HIS
SON, THOM, NOVEMBER 1958

66 To have a father – to be a father – is to come very near the heart of life itself. 99

PRESIDENT RICHARD NIXON, "THE PROCLAMATION OF FATHER'S DAY", MAY 1972

In the Name of the Father

Every year, around the world, families get together on one special day to celebrate dads. Although Mother's Day has been celebrated since the early 1900s, Father's Day was not declared a public holiday in the US until the seventies, when President Richard Nixon officially dedicated "one special Sunday" every year to the role of fathers in society.

Great Britain was quick to follow suit, and the first official Father's Day in the UK and US was held on 18 June 1972.

The Mother of Father's Day

Funnily enough, there was no founding father behind the idea to celebrate dads. In fact, it was down to a woman.

Children's author Sonora Smart Dodd initiated the first ever Father's Day in Spokane, Washington, in 1910 to honour her dad, William Jackson Smart, an American Civil War veteran and single father. Smart raised Dodd and her five younger brothers alone after his wife died in childbirth in 1898.

Twelve years later, Dodd's admiration of her father made her determined to celebrate him, and others like him. And so she convinced local clergymen to hold the first holiday event of its kind, Father's Day. Across the city, sermons were held to honour local men like Smart.

Father's Day was (and still is) held on the third Sunday in June.

Father's Day Traditions Around the World

Mexico: Sign up for a family fun run in honour of Día del Padre.

Thailand: Gift your father a yellow flower called a Canna lily.

Germany: Take your dad on a hiking trip.

France: Gift your father red roses to mark Fête des Pères.

Brazil: Fire up the BBQ for a sumptuous meal with family.

"My father was my teacher. But most importantly he was a great dad."

BEAU BRIDGES, IMDB.COM

" As fathers, we need to be involved in our children's lives not just when it's convenient or easy, and not just when they're doing well – but when it's difficult and thankless, and they're struggling. That is when they need us most. "

BARACK OBAMA, IN AN OPEN LETTER
TO HIS DAUGHTERS, 2009

Dads' Favourite Gifts: Ranked

1. Food and drink (37.66%)
2. Tech (36.66%)
3. Clothing (35.16%)
4. Personalized gifts (32.37%)
5. Fragrance and grooming (30.37%)

FATHER'S DAY DADS SURVEY 2023, CREATE GIFT LOVE

Dad Jokes

Six of the Cheesiest One-liners:

"When does a joke become a dad joke?"

"When it becomes apparent."

"What's the difference between dad jokes and bad jokes?"

"The first letter."

"I love telling dad jokes."

"Sometimes he laughs."

"My dad wanted a groundbreaking gift for Father's Day."

"I bought him a shovel."

"I bought my dad a book about glue once."

"He couldn't put it down."

"Why shouldn't you fundraise for marathons?"

"Because they just take the money and run."

"My kids are my greatest piece of art. If I can pump them full of amazing stuff and surround them with beautiful art and music, then I'm going to live out my life watching them."

JASON MAMOA, IN AN INTERVIEW FOR *MEN'S HEALTH*, 2017

Dad Traits

Height – Dad's height has the most influence on how tall a child will be.

Eye colour – If dad has dominant eye colour genes, a child is likely to inherit their eye colour.

Dental health – Fathers pass on genes that affect the structure of the teeth and jaw.

Hair colour and texture – A father's dominant genes will be a bigger determinant than a mother's.

Gender – It's the father who determines the sex of a baby when either an "X" or "Y" chromosome fertilizes the mother's "X" egg.

DAD'S RECIPE #1

Smashed Burger Tacos

Serves 2
Prep + cook time: 20 minutes

You will need:
17 oz (500 g) beef mince
2 tsp mixed herbs
Pinch of garlic granules
4 mini tortillas
2 mini Gem lettuce
4 slices of burger cheese

Burger sauce:
2 tbsp mayonnaise
1 tbsp tomato sauce
½ tsp English mustard
1 tbsp finely chopped onion
1 tbsp finely chopped gherkin
2 tbsp white wine vinegar

How to make:

- Combine the burger sauce ingredients in a small ramekin.

- In a bowl, roll the beef mince into the garlic granules and mixed herbs, and separate into four burger patties.

- On each tortilla, flatten the beef using your fingers, stretching it right to the edges of the wrap.

- Heat a drizzle of vegetable oil in a pan over a high heat and cook the burger taco meat-side down for 4 minutes.

- Flip the tortilla and cook on the other side for 2 minutes.

- Flip again until the beef is cooked. Add the cheese to melt. Serve with lettuce and burger sauce.

Chapter Two

Dads in History, Myth & Legend

The First Father

The concept of fatherhood in humans is thought to have begun around half a million years ago when an early human species, known as Homo heidelbergensis, learned that staying close to the family after childbirth gave their offspring the best chance of survival.

Suddenly, not only was fatherhood just about reproduction, it was also about protecting the gene pool for future generations and teaching the offspring the vital survival skills they would need for the world around them.

"We have a responsibility and a duty to be fathers, not to just make babies. To be real fathers. And you can't expect any good to come to you if you don't visit any good to your son or your daughter."

DENZEL WASHINGTON, TALKING TO
THE URBAN DADS, 2016

King Bhumibol
(1927–2016)

The late king of Thailand is regarded as the "Father of a nation" after holding the throne for 70 years, the longest reign in the country's history. A symbol of faith, devotion and stability, the king was a beloved national figure.

To this day, Thailand holds their annual Father's Day celebration on the king's birthday (13 October). It is a public holiday, where schools and businesses are closed and citizens wear his favourite colour yellow to honour his memory.

Mahatma Ghandi

(1869–1948)

The father of a different nation, Indian leader Mahatma Ghandi, similarly expanded the notion of family to an entire country. In his later years, after successfully securing independence from British rule in 1947, Ghandi became affectionately known as "Bapu", meaning papa.

His relationship with his own children was not so straightforward. He had four sons, the first of which was born when he was only 18, and who spent a long time separated from his father while Ghandi studied law in London.

Nelson Mandela
(1918–2013)

Freedom fighter Nelson Mandela had six children, but he devoted his life to fighting for his country. In his biography, written when he was 76, he described his "greatest regret" as "watching [his] children grow up without [his] guidance."

On being released from prison after 27 years, Mandela was adopted by the people of South Africa and became the first democratically elected president. His fight for all people is one of the most inspirational in history.

Theodore Roosevelt

(1858–1919)

History may remember Theodore Roosevelt as the 26th President of the United States but at heart, "Teddy" was a devoted family man.

After the heartbreaking sudden death of his first wife, Roosevelt married his childhood friend and they went on to have five children together. Whenever he was apart from his beloved sons and daughters, he would write them heartfelt letters, hundreds of which were published in a bestselling book after his death in 1919.

66 There is no form of happiness on the Earth, no form of success of any kind, that in any way approaches the happiness of the husband and the wife who are married lovers, and the father and mother of plenty of healthy children. 99

THEODORE ROOSEVELT, ESSAY IN *THEODORE ROOSEVELT'S LETTERS TO HIS CHILDREN*, 1919

Prince Albert

(1819–61)

Beloved husband to Queen Victoria, Prince Albert took great pride in raising their nine children.

Victoria and Albert were an outward symbol of domestic bliss. They welcomed five daughters and four sons over 17 years. Albert was heavily involved in their education and in turning their royal estates into comfortable family homes.

In fact, Prince Albert is largely credited with introducing the Christmas Tree to the UK in 1840. Today, it is the focal point and a symbol of family and unity in most British households during the festive season.

Sporting Heroes #1

*Bronny &
LeBron James*

At the age of 39, basketball legend LeBron James added to his unbelievable NBA legacy when his 19-year-old son, Bronny, was drafted for the same basketball team LeBron has played on for seven years, the LA Lakers.

Never in history had a father and son duo played together in an NBA game until 23 October 2024.

"I've learned that the simplest things in life – like having a minute with [my children] – are worth more than any painting, any photograph, any house or any hit record."

ELTON JOHN, IN AN INTERVIEW WITH *THE MIRROR*, 2016

"I did the first nappy. It was a badge of honour. I had every midwife staring at me."

PRINCE WILLIAM, IN AN INTERVIEW WITH CNN, 2013

Sporting Heroes #2

Kasper & Peter Schmeichel

Peter Schmeichel is considered the best football player in Danish history, playing in goal in no less than 129 games for his national team. So, imagine his pride when son Kasper followed in his footsteps to become goalkeeper for Denmark, too.

Schmeichel Sr played for Manchester United until his retirement in 2003. His son – 23 years his junior – now plays professionally for Leicester City.

Record Breakers #1

Ngim Chhamji &
Dendi Sherpa

Dendi Sherpa was on top of the world when he reached the peak of Mount Everest with his 16-year-old daughter Chhamji in May 2012. Together, they became Guinness World Record holders for the first father and daughter to reach the highest point on Earth.

The proud dad also got to see his daughter achieve two records simultaneously, as she was also the youngest female to summit Everest (south side). Peak fatherhood!

66 **She did not stand alone, but what stood behind her, the most potent moral force in her life, was the love of her father.** **99**

HARPER LEE, *GO SET A WATCHMAN*, 2015

Record Breakers #2

Mykolas &
Virgilijus Alenka

If anyone is going to beat your record, you'd want it to be your child. That's exactly what discus thrower Mykolas Alenka did just a few months before the Paris Olympics 2024, when he shattered the longest-standing world record in men's athletics with a throw of 74.34m.

His father, Virgilijus, previously held the Olympic record of 69.89m, which Mykolas matched at the 2024 Games.

"Time goes by so fast. One minute you're holding them for the first time in hospital, the next they're driving their car. But it's so special – I wouldn't change it for the world."

DAVID BECKHAM, IN AN
INTERVIEW FOR UNICEF, 2018

Odin & Thor

Norse mythology

A powerhouse duo: Odin is regarded as the All-Father of the gods while his son Thor (as Marvel fans will know) is an unstoppable hammer-wielding force.

Dagda & Aengus

Celtic mythology

In a tale of betrayal, Aengus tricks his father, Dagda, into granting him sole ownership of the family home after learning that it was promised to his siblings.

"Few sons indeed are like their fathers; most are worse, few better than their fathers."

HOMER, *THE ODYSSEY*, 1614

Odysseus & Telemachus

Greek mythology

Engrained in Homer's ancient Greek epic *The Odyssey* is a son's unwavering belief that he will be reunited with his father, who has gone off to fight the Trojan War.

Zeus & Cronus

Greek mythology

Here, a father's fear of being overthrown by his own children drives him to swallow them whole. Ultimately, the prophecy comes true when Zeus and his siblings return to fight Cronus for the throne.

King Polybus & Oedipus

Greek mythology

In the ancient Greek tragedy *Oedipus Rex*, the king of Corinth, Polybus, adopts an abandoned child and raises him as his own. Later, when Oedipus is ordered to kill his father, he kills Polybus, not realizing he had never actually met his biological father.

"An almost perfect relationship with his father was the earthly root of all his wisdom."

C.S. LEWIS, *PHANTASTES*, 1858

Osiris and Horus

Egyptian mythology

Horus sets out to avenge the death of the father he never met. Osiris was the king of Egypt until he was killed by his own brother, Set, who usurped the throne.

Atticus Finch

To Kill A Mockingbird (1960)
Book by Harper Lee

Raising two children as a single working father, Atticus Finch does his best to teach Jem and Scout integrity and strong values.

Looking from the outside into a happy, loving home, we get to see a different parenting dynamic in 1930s America to the typical stay-at-home mother and absent father.

As a father figure, Atticus' approach is cool and collected. He doesn't yell, but always tries to see things from his child's perspective.

Chris Gardner

The Pursuit of Happyness (2007) Film based on Chris Gardner's autobiographical book

In everything that he does, Chris Gardner is motivated by a brighter future for himself and his four-year-old son.

As a father, he tries to protect Christopher Jr from his mother walking out and their increasingly dire living situation. They are homeless and broke, but they are together.

Mufasa

The Lion King (1994)
Film directed by Roger Allers
& Rob Minkoff

In the kill-or-be-killed animal kingdom, the best a father like Mufasa can do is show his children how to be brave.

And, by the time Simba is old enough to have a pride of his own, the lion fearlessly faces up to his evil uncle and has clearly remembered everything his father taught him about fighting fair.

Finding Nemo (2003)
Film directed by Andrew Stanton

When Nemo is accidentally separated from his parents at birth, new dad Marlin is driven to the ends of the ocean to find his lost son.

Though he has to step out of his comfort zone and face some pretty extreme challenges, there is nothing this dad wouldn't do to make sure his child is safe.

Uncle Phil

The Fresh Prince of Bel-Air (1990–6)
TV series by Andy and Susan Borowitz

Lovable disciplinarian Uncle Phil took in nephew Will and looked after him like his own son.

Even though they didn't always see eye-to-eye — and the teenager was constantly getting into trouble — Uncle Phil stepped up where Will's own father fell down. He gave him a room in his palatial home and kept him out of trouble, doing his best to share the kind of morals and wisdom that would make a boy into a man.

❝You have a little girl, an adorable little girl, who looks up to you and adores you in a way you could never have imagined. I remember how her little hand used to fit inside mine... She said I was her hero.❞

GEORGE BANKS (PLAYED BY STEVE MARTIN), IN *FATHER OF THE BRIDE*, 1991

George Banks

Father of the Bride (1991)
Film directed by Charles Shyer

As he prepares to watch his daughter Annie walk down the aisle, George Banks is dealing with a fear most fathers of daughters can relate to: being replaced. He seems to have blinked and his little girl is all grown up, ready to move out and start a family of her own.

Fans who followed the family into the sequel also got to see George's shock when he learned he was going to be a new dad again at 45, just as he was expecting his first grandchild.

Santa Claus

No-one really knows if Father Christmas has any children of his own, but he sure does like to make our children happy. The legend of Santa dates back to Christian bishop Saint Nicholas, who was known for his generosity. Today, he is a jolly father figure to all, symbolizing festive cheer.

The benefits of playing this legendary figure are many: from being left a drink with mince pie at midnight to having a good excuse for showing off an over-indulged belly. But whether or not your little ones still believe that one man can deliver that many presents, you will be grateful for the threat of the "Naughty or Nice" list!

Bandit

Bluey (2018–present)
TV series created by Joe Brumm

This generation of dads can't move for parenting lessons they can take from canine patriarch Bandit. He represents the modern man, who plays an equal part in entertaining, guiding and understanding his two daughters with their mother, Chilli.

The creator wrote the episodes while he was working from home and raising his son, saying that he wanted to help dads realize they are "just as important as mums".

Daniel Hilliard

Mrs Doubtfire (1993)
Film directed by Chris Columbus

When desperate dad Daniel Hilliard slips into a wig, tights and prosthetics to pose as an English nanny vying for his estranged family's new housekeeper position, he proved that he would stop at nothing to see his three children.

The eccentric dad even manages to scare off their would-be stepfather in the process. Job done.

Advice for Dads from Fictional Fathers

"A good dad stays positive no matter how much you want to scream."
Bob Cratchit, *A Christmas Carol* by Charles Dickens

"Bad language is a stage all children go through, and it dies with time when they learn they're not attracting attention with it."
Atticus Finch, *To Kill A Mockingbird* by Harper Lee

"Know your strengths as a father and what you can bring to the table without rocking the boat."
Mathew Cuthbert, *Anne of Green Gables* by Lucy Maud Montgomery

70

"I'm not a brilliant man, but I can tell you the key to being a good father figure is not getting involved with the punishments. Be the gentle giant that a child can lean on."
Joe Gargery, *Great Expectations* by Charles Dickens

"Give your children what they need emotionally, or they will seek it out elsewhere."
Jean Valjean, *Les Misérables* by Victor Hugo

Chapter Three

Dads of the Animal Kingdom

Universal Role Models

In the animal world, the role of a father is incredibly varied, as it is for humans. Sometimes it's similar to the more traditional paternal role of the protector: teaching, playing with and providing for the family are all a key part of lion and ape daddy duties. While in other species, dads are can be extremely hands-on: incubating, feeding and even giving birth to the offspring can be a part of their role!

Now that's shared parental responsibility!

"A father's goodness is *higher than the mountain,* **A mother's goodness** *deeper than the sea.***"**

JAPANESE PROVERB

Mountain Gorilla

Average number of children:
10–20 infants over a lifetime.

Baby name: Infant.

Newborn size: 4.5lbs (2kg).

The silverback gorilla is a fierce protector, a hands-on dad and a loyal partner. He hunts for the whole troop (typically up to 50lbs of food per head, per day) but always shares it with the mother of his children first.

He is playful with his infants but must remain vigilant, defending them from the attack of rival male gorillas. Usually, he sticks around until they reach early adulthood.

Wolf

Average number of children:
4–6 pups per litter.

Baby name: Pup.

Newborn size: 16oz (45g).

Male wolves truly embody the "father figure" dynamic.

Fathers, grandfathers, uncles and brothers all play a part in parental care for the young pups.

An older wolf always shares the responsibility as the protector of the breeding den – where female wolves go to give birth – even if they are not the paternal father.

After birth, wolves stay around to help feed, protect and play with their pups.

Emperor Penguin

Average number of children:
One egg per year.

Baby name: Chick.

Newborn size: 11oz (315g).

Penguin dads step up straight after the mother lays an egg.

His role is long and extremely important, as he is tasked with keeping the egg incubated between his legs in the freezing Antarctic temperatures while the mother gets back to full health.

For two bitter months, the father faces extreme hunger and 100mph winds while he struggles to stay in one spot.

African Wild Dog

Average number of children:
10–12 pups per litter.

Baby name: Pup.

Newborn size: Not recorded.

As anyone who has ever looked after a new dog will know, puppies are hard work.

With plenty of energy and a hearty appetite, wild dog pups keep dads on their toes from the word go.

Dad has to be the sole feeder, even in the first 10 weeks when the pups can't eat solids; his only option is to chew the food first and serve it to them soft.

Flamingo

Average number of children: One per year.

Baby name: Chick.

Newborn size: 2.5oz (70g).

Male flamingos are ultimate feminists.

Not only do they stay monogamous when surrounded by thousands of other potential mates, but they also split all parenting duties down the middle.

Even though they can't carry the egg themselves, they help to find a suitable nesting site then build the nest, with their mate, out of mud. After the birth, the parents take it in turns to incubate the egg and keep it safe.

Frog

Average number of children:
Up to 4,000 eggs every spring
(only two may survive to
adulthood).

Baby name: Tadpole.

Newborn size: Around 12mm.

You might not understand a frog's approach to parenting, but you have to respect it.

Once a mother has laid her eggs, a father will watch them until they become tadpoles and then... swallow them. By keeping them in his vocal sac, he provides a warm, moist and oxygenated environment suitable for them to flourish into frogs. That's when they hop out and start life.

Doves

Average number of children:
Around 10–12 eggs per season.

Baby name: Squab.

Newborn weight: Under 1lb (450g).

In some bird species, the father can play a leading role in infant feeding.

Dove dads start producing "crop milk" two days before a mother's eggs are due to hatch so that he can help to feed the squabs for the first five days.

Much like human milk, the protein-rich food helps to improve the squabs' chances of survival and helps them grow rapidly.

Fox

Average number of children:
Around 4–6 cubs per litter.

Baby name: Cub.

Newborn weight: 3.4oz (96g).

Fox fathers play a huge role in providing food for the family, while the mother nests at home with her babies.

When the cubs are old enough, a father will teach them how to hunt for themselves by cunningly hiding food near the family den and sending them out to find it. They must follow their own noses and learn how to forage.

Lion

Average number of children:
Around 18 cubs over a lifetime.

Baby name: Cub.

Newborn weight: 4.1lbs (1.65kg).

A pride is a unique type of extra-large family made up of females, cubs and a coalition of males.

However, if *The Lion King* taught us anything, it's that a lion is not even safe around his family.

In his role as fierce protector, a father teaches his young by example: showing them dominance, submission and cooperation by the way he acts.

SEAHORSE

Average number of children:
Around 200 at a time.

Baby name: Fry.

Newborn weight: Under 0.5oz (1g).

Did you know seahorses are one of the only male species on earth to experience pregnancy?

In a case of total role reversal, the mother deposits her eggs in a pouch on the front of the father's body where he fertilizes and keeps them safe.

Forty-five days later, he goes into labour and gives birth to tiny seahorses. Almost straight away, he can be pregnant again.

And Finally, the WORST Animal Dads

- **The cannibal:** Iguana eat their own defenceless young when food stocks are low.

- **The defector:** Shortly after the eggs have spawned, most sea bass dads will swim away.

- **The lazy one:** Goby fish deliberately try to reduce their workload the moment a mother's back is turned by eating some of the eggs.

The good-for-nothing: Gelada Monkeys do virtually nothing to help mothers rear children.

The one with the bad temper: Chimps are known to fly off the handle and attack other chimps, especially little ones.

The grizzly one: The grizzly bear, you guessed it, likes to leave a solitary life, leaving the mother with the responsibility of raising the cubs. At worse, they are known to, on rare occasions, even kill or eat them!

Chapter Four

The Modern Dad

"When you meet your kids you realize that they deserve great parents. And then you have your marching orders, and you have to try and become the person that they deserve."

RYAN GOSLING, IN AN
INTERVIEW WITH *GQ*, 2016

Dads Today

Plenty has changed about what it means to be a great dad today. It doesn't necessarily mean working all hours to bring home food and money for the family anymore. The modern dad knows that providing for a family can include everything from doing the school drop-offs to showing up at sports day. It means reading to the children before bedtime and making their breakfast in the morning.

So, what does a modern dad look like?

The Birth of a Father

If you're a new dad, welcome to the world! Right now, you will be riding an emotional rollercoaster, but by the time you get off, you will say it was the best ride in the park.

Remember, it's not just the mothers who get hit with the lows. Did you know that men get postpartum depression (PPD), too?

As many as 1 in 10 men struggle with depression and anxiety in the first six months of having a child, so it is just as important to look after yourself as your baby and partner.

Hey, it's OK!

Useful Everyday Mantras for New Dads:

"I am good enough."

**"I am doing everything
I can, and it is everything
my family needs."**

**"I am grateful, and my
family is grateful for me."**

**"I believe in myself
and my abilities."**

"My baby is safe. My baby is warm. My baby is loved."

"By taking care of myself, I am caring for my family."

"Nothing in life is permanent. This too shall pass."

"My family are lucky to have me."

"I am lucky to have my family."

"Every dad is learning as they go."

The Love Hormone

Fatherhood literally changes the biology of a man. We know that women experience a spike in hormones during childbirth – specifically the love hormone oxytocin – but researchers recently discovered that men get a similar spike over the first six months of fatherhood, helping them to bond with their babies.

Around the same time, testosterone decreases, improving fathers' receptiveness to infant signals like crying.

"It's a different kind of love. It's very pure. It's unconditional, but they haven't earned it yet. They didn't do anything. They just exist."

JOHN LEGEND, ON *THE LATE SHOW WITH STEPHEN COLBERT*, 2017

DAD'S RECIPE #2

The New "Old Fashioned" Cocktail

Serves 1
Prep time: 4–6 minutes

You will need:
2oz (55g) bourbon whisky
1 tsp maple syrup (*for a sweeter taste)
2 dashes of orange bitters
Ice cubes
Orange peel
1 cocktail cherry

How to make:

▶ Stir the bourbon, bitters and maple syrup together in a lowball glass.

▶ Swirl with large ice cubes for 20 seconds to chill the drink.

▶ Serve with orange peel and a cocktail cherry for decoration.

Fatherhood at 50

The paternal age for dads is on the rise. The oldest recorded father (Ramjit Raghav from India) was 94 when he had his first baby. He had a second two years later, and lived to 104.

In the US, the average age of fatherhood has risen from 30 to 32. More men are becoming dads in their fifties, too. By this age, men are more likely to have achieved career success and satisfaction, have formed stronger relationships and be earning more money.

"I want [my children] to be happy. I want them to have a sense of humour. I want them to be interested in things. I want them to be compassionate about other people's plights."

GEORGE CLOONEY, IN AN INTERVIEW WITH *THE HOLLYWOOD REPORTER*, 2017

The "Dad Bod" is Scientific Fact

Becoming a dad will make you gain weight. Science says so. Apparently, the average dad can expect his BMI to increase by 2.6 per cent (that's roughly 4.4lbs/2kg). It's slightly less (2 per cent) if they live outside the family home, but the evidence is there.

Compared to men who don't have children, the average 6-foot (1.8m) tall man will actually lose 1.4lbs (635g) over the same 20-year period.

Scientists have speculated about whether parents buy more highly calorific foods, or if men become less proactive in their healthy habits, such as going to the gym. (Either way, it seems that you're not the only one!)

Two Dads are Better Than One

More and more children are thriving in same-sex families where they have not just one dad, but two! Recent findings show that these children do just as well emotionally, socially and educationally as their peers.

Ever since 2005, two dads have been eligible to adopt together in the UK, and it is now legal in all 50 US states. Both men also have the right to be named on a child's birth certificate.

... and Many Dads are Better Than None!

They say it takes a village! Well, in some tribes of the Amazon, nearly all children will be raised by more than one father. The concept is known as "partible paternity", where several men may take responsibility for a newborn, believing it takes more than one partner to nurture new life.

Not only does this approach support the mother, it increases the survival chances of the infant.

Child's Play

Ever noticed how dads play a little differently with their kids, compared to mothers? Tickling. Chasing. Play-fighting. Well, rough-and-tumble play is more than just a bit of fun for big kids.

In fact, research suggests it could be hugely important for a child's development. Studies have shown that playful behaviours like wrestling, grappling and tumbling can improve social competence and emotional regulation.

Balancing the Books

You might think that reading the football scores out loud is just an old habit, but for children, seeing their father read is believed to be hugely beneficial.

Not only does it improve the emotional and physical connection between father-and-child, it helps to break the assumption (especially for boys) that only females read, since female teachers and mothers are the most likely figures to read to them at a young age.

Right Here, Right Now

Dads today spend triple the amount of time with their children than their own dads did. Millennial dads (those born between 1981 and 1996) are taking a significantly bigger role in childcare than previous generations, whether it's bath times, school drop-offs or early parental leave.

Since the pandemic, remote working has improved parents' flexibility, but research also shows that modern fathers *want* to spend more time with their children.

Countries with the Best Paternity Leave

Men who take parental leave are more likely to be actively involved throughout their children's lives. Here's how work policies compare around the world:

1.	South Korea	548 days
2.	Japan	365 days
3.	Sweden	240 days
4.	Iceland	183 days
5.	Finland	160 days
6.	Spain	112 days
7.	Bulgaria	60 days
8.	France	28 days
9.	Greece	14 days
10.	UK	14 days
11.	USA	0 days

❝Men should always change diapers. It's a very rewarding experience. It's mentally cleansing. It's like washing dishes.❞

CHRIS MARTIN, IN AN INTERVIEW WITH *BLENDER MAGAZINE*, 2008

The Rise of the Stay-at-home Dad

The role of the modern dad is shifting. In a reversal of traditional family dynamics, more and more men are choosing to stay at home and take on the majority of care for the children while their partners pursue their careers and earn money for the family.

In Finland, after being handed a generous nine weeks off work at 70 per cent pay after the birth of a child, the average father goes on to spend more time with their school-age children each day than their mothers.

Stepping Up

Stepdads are sometimes the unsung heroes of the family, but it takes a special man to help raise a child. Around 16.5 million men have stepped up to the role of stepdad in America. In the UK, one in six men in their 30s is a stepfather. Not only does it provide support for the other parent, it creates a safe and supported home environment in which children thrive, not to mention a bond that can last a lifetime.

"When someone takes you on as their own when you're not biologically their own, I think is really special... [My stepdad] didn't have to raise me. *He wanted to.***"**

JONATHAN VAN NESS, "IT'S BEEN A MINUTE"
PODCAST WITH SAM SANDERS, 2019

The Role of Grandfathers

Some dads see grandparenting as a chance to do it all again. Another shot at shaping little humans, perhaps this time with a little more pause for thought. It's even been shown that grandparents who regularly look after their children will live longer!

For a child, grandparents provide wisdom and stability, improving feelings of security and often teaching them essential resilience and coping skills.

10 Rookie Mistakes a Dad Will Only Make Once

☑ Falling asleep in the delivery room (it doesn't go down well).

☑ Taking your time with a nappy (you're in the splash zone!).

☑ Comparing yourself to others (everyone "dads" differently).

☑ Forgetting to pack snacks (for you, as much as for them).

☑ Taking the lid off anything for them (they like to do it themselves).

☑ Agreeing to screens at the table (do it once, do it forever).

A Hand for the Single Dads

To the dads who are doing it alone, raising children as both "mother" and "father" – you are doing an amazing job.

Children don't always see the pain or the strife, but if what they see is a man who shows up, fights fires and keeps them safe, then what they will see is a superhero.

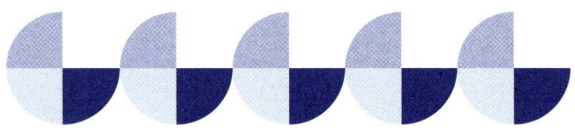

"There's no one I'd rather be with than my kids."

RALPH LAUREN, IN AN INTERVIEW
WITH OPRAH WINFREY, 2011

Make Each Day Count

In parenting, they say: "The days are long but the years are short." You treasure the moment they were born like it was yesterday. The joy. The hope... The FEAR. You can blink and it will feel like a distant memory. Like everything, fatherhood is filled with its ups and downs, yet somehow the memories that stay with us are the amazing ones. Whether you're a seasoned parent or you're just getting started, make every day count.

Fatherhood is a gift.